John George Cragg

Heavy Trail Balances Made Easy

John George Cragg

Heavy Trail Balances Made Easy

ISBN/EAN: 9783744692830

Printed In Europe, USA, Canada, Australia, Japan

Cover: Foto ©ninafisch / pixelio.de

More available books at **www.hansebooks.com**

HEAVY TRIAL BALANCES MADE EASY.

A New Method to Secure the Immediate
Agreement of Trial Balances without
Trouble.

———

ILLUSTRATED BY COLOURED EXAMPLES.

———

BY

J. G. CRAGGS, F.C.A.

(Of the Firm of Craggs, Turketine & Co., Chartered Accountants,
52, Coleman Street, London, E.C.)

LONDON: THE SCIENTIFIC PRESS, LIMITED,

28 & 29, Southampton Street, Strand, W.C.

1897.

TABLE OF CONTENTS.

ILLUSTRATIONS AND EXAMPLES.

PREFACE.

THE system of ensuring the agreement of Trial Balances which this book explains has been in use by my firm for 15 or 16 years. Though the primary idea upon which it is based is very simple—when discovered !—yet it was only after experiencing very great difficulties in complex and voluminous accounts, and especially in connection with one very comprehensive audit, that this idea was originated and the system developed with the assistance of Mr. Hayter, one of our clerks.

Partly owing to its simplicity and partly to the usual exigencies of "calling over" the adoption of the new method takes no extra time whatever; it only utilises time at present wasted when "calling over," and yet at the same operation co-ordinates the figures so as to give any desired results.

It is of the greatest value where the accounts are very heavy, and also where the operations of the business concerned do not naturally fall into such sub-divisions as can be readily followed by isolating the books of account to agree with them. At first we only used the system for heavy accounts, but

many years' experience has led us to adopt it
wherever there is a likelihood of there being
difficulties in agreeing the books at a stocktaking.

I have recently made this new method public by
a Lecture, entitled "The Agreement of Trial
Balances Simplified and Secured by a New
Method," which was delivered to the Edinburgh
Chartered Accountants Students' Society, at a
Meeting held on the 14th November, 1895, and
this work is partly taken from that Lecture.

J. G. CRAGGS.

52, Coleman Street, E.C.,
    November 2nd, 1896.

HEAVY TRIAL BALANCES MADE EASY—A NEW METHOD.

GENERAL EXPLANATION.

Every responsible person, whose duty it is to obtain the agreement by trial balance of a considerable number of transactions recorded in books of account, fully realises what an anxious time has to be gone through when a precise agreement has to be obtained at a Stocktaking, and some tantalising difference occurs, which, in spite of the exercise of the greatest ingenuity, continues for a long time, and perhaps altogether, to baffle research. The mental wear and tear on such occasions is too well appreciated by those for whom this book is intended to need any description at my hands, and this worry is frequently aggravated by the anxiety of the partners or the directors, as the case may be, to ascertain, and it may be, to report to Shareholders, the results of the business for the given period without delay. Of course the results, subject to an agreement, may be furnished, but it is usually a bad plan to prepare the final accounts before the books are precisely agreed, as in most cases if the difference in agreement be once left it tends to be left always.

From earliest times it has been well known that while it is impossible to break a given bundle of sticks when bound together, yet if unbound, and each stick taken separately, the whole can be easily broken. This New Method proceeds upon similar lines, but in that respect there is nothing new in it, as it has always been the aim of Accountants and expert Book-keepers to sub-divide the agreement of their books as much as possible. What, however, is done by the New Method is to make as many sub-divisions as may be desired, with the greatest ease, and to vary them at any time during a given period, all without the slightest necessity for making artificial barriers between any of the books, which has been the manner usually adopted hitherto. The whole separation into separate "sticks" (if I may be permitted to use the before-mentioned classical illustration) is arrived at *independently and outside of any of the books of account*, which are left so free that even if it were desirable in, say, a trading concern, to post from any Country Day Book to the Bought Ledger, the Private Ledger, or even the Cash Book, as well as to the Country Ledger, it could be done without in any way affecting the ultimate agreement or localisation of the transaction to its proper quarter.

In order to apply the system it is only necessary (1) to do that which is done in every properly conducted Counting House, viz :—**Call Back the Entries in the Books,** (which can of course be done either by the Counting House Clerks or by the Auditor,) and (2) to arrange that when this is being done the clerk who calls from the Day Book or Journal, instead of being idle while the other clerk is finding the account in the Ledger, **puts down the amount only** in a column of a special book provided for that purpose, and which is called a Slip Book.

Assuming the calling is from Day Books to various Ledgers, as one Ledger would be called at a time, the total of the entries made in the column would be the total of such entries going into the particular Ledger. This being carried throughout the calling over of the books, and summarised at the end of the period up to which the books are balanced, would furnish the separate debit and

credit totals, or the balances (as may be required)
that should be shown by each respective Ledger, no
matter how numerous may be the Ledgers in use.

All this will be fully shown in the detailed
explanation which shortly follows, but in the meantime the reader's attention is called to the very
important fact above demonstrated that the New
Method involves **no extra time whatever,** the time
occupied by the one clerk in writing down the amount
being at most not more than the time occupied by
the other clerk in finding the place in the Ledger.
The only expense incidental to the New Method is
that of the paper and ink needed for taking down
the figures, which is a trifle. The additions of the
items have to be made in the slip books, but the
checking of the additions in the actual books of
account is saved, and as the castings of the slip books,
thus independently made, must agree with the total
in the books of account, no error can be passed over
by careless checking or oversight due to a badly
made or badly placed figure. Even if the " New
Method " should in any exceptional case need some
extra time (which can be but slight), the certainty
of rapid agreement at balancing coupled with the
fact that such extra work is distributed over each
month, ensures such relief from pressure at stock-

taking, when of course the work is heaviest, that its adoption is fully warranted in spite of such conditions.

There is given later on some extracts from the Lecture upon this subject and other comments, which contain several useful points and suggestions as well as some reference to important advantages that arise out of the adoption of the "New Method," but in the meantime the foregoing general remarks will have made clear to the reader the main idea of the system, and it will be easy for him to comprehend the detailed description which follows showing how the system is applied in actual practice.

DESCRIPTION OF "NEW METHOD."

As all books of account, no matter how named,
how numerous, or how diversified, resolve themselves into two classes, viz : Journals and Ledgers—
the former taking the transactions in the order of
time that they arise, and the latter analysing them
according to their nature under different headings
and accounts—it will be more convenient for the
purposes of illustration to speak only of the Journal
and Ledger, except where the context or the subject
illustrated requires otherwise. The reader will
perhaps kindly bear this in mind, and that though
only the terms "Journal" and "Ledger" may be
used, the system is applicable to all books and all
businesses, even to "Stock-jobbers'" accounts
where a Journal properly so called is apt to be
missing.

It must be supposed that two clerks are about to
check the postings from the Journals to the Ledgers,
one clerk takes a ledger the other a journal, but
under the new system the Journalman, in addition
to the journal before him, would have by his side a
book ruled simply with money columns. (See

illustration No. 2). Preferably this should be a
foolscap book with a limp cover, or one that can be
easily bent back, so that it need take up very little
room. As the Journalman is only using one column
at a time, so long as that one column is visible it
will be enough, and he may cover other parts of the
slip book by the Journal with which he is working.
Hence no appreciable extra working room is required,
a point which is often of importance. As many
money columns are put on a page of foolscap as
may suit the importance of the entries dealt with;
if the amounts are heavy, fewer columns, and if
light more columns.

The clerks then proceed to call over by the
following routine :—

No. 1.—ORDER OF CALLING WHEN TAKING DOWN.

1.—J. (The *Journalman*) calls the folio, name,
and address.

2.—*J., whilst waiting for L. (the Ledgerman) to find
the place, writes the amount in a column in
the Slip Book.*

3.—L., having found the folio, calls back name
and address.

4.—J. calls the item and ticks it.

5.—L. calls back the item and ticks in Ledger.

6.—*J. looks at item* IN SLIP BOOK *as L. calls it back.*

It is of considerable importance that this routine should be followed exactly in the order in which it is given above, so as to secure accuracy in the work done. If it is not so done, misunderstandings may arise, and errors be passed over, for it is much easier for an error to be passed over in calling than is usually imagined. There is nearly always some cause or reason for an error, and such cause or reason is just as likely to exercise an influence when calling over as when the error originated.

It will be observed that when the ledgerman calls back the figures (rule 5) it is the duty of the journal-man to look, not at the corresponding item in the actual book of account from which he first read it aloud, *but at the item in the slip book* and see if he has written it down correctly, for this reason he ticks the item in the Journal *when he calls it*, instead of waiting to do so, as in the ordinary course, until the Ledgerman has called it back.

No. 2.—TAKING DOWN, or SLIP BOOK.

This is the all-important illustration for shewing the new system. The money columns which occupy

Breaks—136 and 141.

C. 6 contd.			C. 7			175	14	5	C. 3			176	12	4	C. 2			T. 2		
166	18	3	4	0	0	5	17	2	2	2	0	1	11	10	1	18	0	(136)		
13	17	7	2	10	0	6	0	0	1	12	4	1	19	5	2	4	5			
4	15	8	3	14	7	7	12	4	4	13	9	2	17	10	1	1	2	3	5	8
3	7	0	8	16	4	4	10	0	3	17	0	10	0	0	5	1	3			
11	7	1	2	13	0	1	12	6	12	17	11	1	1	0	10	4	10	(141)		
20	0	9	0	0	4	10	0	0	0	2	3	7	9	5	(136)			3	5	8
2	11	0	7	9	4	12	3	3	0	18	0	7	6	8						
4	18	9	3	17	0	3	9	11	12	14	2	13	18	0	14	4	11			
4	2	6	7	5	0	16	4	0	0	1	2	25	0	10	9	9	6			
9	0	0	0	1	3	1	6	6	0	0	4	1	10	1	6	12	0			
0	12	0	3	17	1	2	7	8	18	6	10	1	18	9	3	0	9			
15	0	0	2	6	1	1	17	10	20	0	0 (1)	7	14	0	(141)					
3	2	4	3	7	0	13	0	0	10	5	10	11	7	8	43	12	0			
3	0	0	0	0	2				3	5	0	8	0	0						
1	15	0	1	13	0	(141)			11	14	9	4	19	0						
5	16	11	3	19	6				0	1	6	1	19	0						
1	4	0	6	1	9	261	15	7	2	6	6	2	10	4						
4	5	0	1	1	6				6	5	4	1	2	0						
2	5	1	4	15	6				20	0	0	0	0	2						
29	5	3	15	16	4				0	0	7	11	2	0						
			20	8	0				16	15	8	0	16	6						
(141)			1	10	0				6	3	6	3	1	10						
			48	8	1				1	14	6	5	4	0						
306	19	2	1	18	6				0	0	2	0	1	0						
			7	10	10				155	19	2	20	0	0						
			8	19	11				(136)			4	11	0						
			4	16	10				3	11	10	6	1	6						
			3	17	6				4	19	1	5	4	0						
			(136)						12	2	3	(141)								
			175	14	5				176	12	4	346	0	2						

SUMMARIES.
August, 1885.

Town	2	3	5	8	8 5 8
Country	1	9	9	3	
„	2	43	12	0	
„	3	346	0	2	
New „	4	1543	1	8	
Old „	4	52	10	10	
„	5	18	14	6	
„	6	306	19	2	
„	7	261	15	7	
„	8	266	19	4	2849 2 6
		2852	8	2	2852 8 2

fully every page are simply ordinary red money
columns, without head-lines. In this particular
case you will observe that they have evidently been
"calling" some book which is called "Small Day
Book," and that when they started the page shown
in this illustration they were engaged in calling the
entries to the Country Ledger No. 6. There were
apparently some twenty more items in the Day Book
for this No. 6. Ledger, and when these were done,
141 was, for reasons given later, put at the bottom,
and No. 7 Ledger was then fetched. A salutary
rule is, that while one clerk is occupied in getting a
fresh Ledger, or in any other way, the other clerk is
not to waste his time (or rather his employer's), but
is to do some of the additions in the Slip Book, or
similar work.

It is evident that 141 indicates the end of the
month in the Day Book, because at this point they
go on to Ledger 7. "Breaks 136 and 141" on the
top of the book will be explained presently, but in
the meantime we follow the two clerks at their work.
The journalman goes back to the beginning of the
month (August 1885) in the Day Book, and commences to call to Ledger 7. They call straight
away all the items they find there, and consequently
when they get them all down, the Slip Book gives

them the total of the items in this Day Book affecting Ledger 7, which in this example was £261 15s. 7d.
Still looking at Ledger 7, you see, at the foot of the
first column of items called, the figures 136.   The
journalman does not stop here, however, but goes on
to 141, which must be the last page in the Day Book
for the month, as you will observe that here also the
total is carried to the summary shewn in the corner
of the illustration.

The castings are made afterwards, or at any convenient moment that fits in with other work; of
course they are not done at the time of calling, or it
would keep the ledgerman waiting.   The clerks then
appear to have passed on to the Country Ledger No. 3,
then Country Ledger No. 2, and finally they have to
get Town Ledger No. 2, as there was one item for
that department.

Having evidently completed this Day Book, the
"summary" shown on the right hand is made,
and this should be considered very carefully.   The
figures demonstrate that as many as ten Ledgers
have been affected by the entries in this Small Day
Book.

The total of £2852 8s. 2d. having been agreed
with the additions in the Day Book itself, is inserted
in ink, and finally the clerks know by this system

into what amounts this total was sub-divided between these ten Ledgers. Small sums are mostly used in the illustrations for simplicity's sake.

Think for a moment of the wide spreading effect of this. **There are ten Ledgers affected by one Day Book,** and except for this system all these must have been agreed in one lump, but by separating them the difficulties of agreement are reduced to *one-tenth only*.

Looking again at this summary it may be observed that an item of £3 5s. 8d. has been entered wrongly by the entering clerk. It should have gone into a Town Day Book, and not a Country Day Book. The summary, therefore, shows that out of the total debits—£2852 8s. 2d.—a sum of £3 5s. 8d. affects the town department, and the balance of £2849 2s. 6d. affects the country department. It does not, however, upset the work; the clerks put down Town Ledger 2, and it goes in its right place.

Another great convenience of this system is illustrated by the Country Ledger No. 4, shown in this summary. In this case there is a New Country No. 4, and an Old Country No. 4. Thus, it is apparent that the new method is not bound to any special sub-divisions fixed upon a long time beforehand, but can be divided as wished at the moment. Doubtless the old ledger was kept on until the accounts therein gradually cleared themselves up, so that ultimately there were only a few balances to transfer. A good many readers may have experienced the trouble of going through an old ledger, perhaps very full of accounts, and which are very often written one under the other on any chance space the Ledger-keeper may have discovered, only possibly to find in the whole ledger a few balances or entries here and there, and those who have had this experience will realise how easily a balance or an entry may be overlooked. By the Slip Books, however, any such an omission can be easily detected. Here only £52 10s. 10d. went into the old Ledger in the month, and as the Ledgers are supposed to contain 1000 pages each, it is like looking for a needle in a haystack.

A reference has already been made to what are called "breaks" when referring to the words "Breaks 136 and 141," which appear on the top of the page in illustration No. 2, and these require explanation.

It is agreed before the clerks commence to call a Journal that they will mark "breaks" at such and such pages. It often happens, in the case of heavy

accounts, that there may be perhaps 100 pages of
Day Book to the month ; and if the total of the
Slip Books for that month differ from the Day Book
total the error could not without "breaks" be located
to any part of these 100 pages. Suppose, then, that
before commencing to work upon such a Day Book it
is agreed to make a break or stoppage for additions,
say at the end of every fifth page of the Day Book.
The clerks should then note at the top of the Slip
Books such breaks, for instance, as—136, 141,
146, 151, and so on. This keeps the journalman
informed at what particular points to stop for a
moment, and his memory is further assisted by
putting a piece of blotting paper or other mark into
the book at the break he is next coming to. When
he comes to a break, all he does is to skip a few lines
in his Slip Book, and put the folio in a ring, as shown
in the example. If he attempts to do more he might
keep the ledgerman waiting. By the foregoing means
the men who are calling are able to prove the total
of the Slip Book up to any individual break. As
the Slip Books must necessarily contain the entries
in the order that they are called to each Ledger,
whilst the Day Book takes them chronologically, it
it is clear that unless the figures going to each
Ledger are all strictly marked at each break, it

might be necessary to go over the whole of the
castings in both Day Book and Slip Book if they
did not agree.   Of course, as a matter of practice, if
there were say 100 pages of Day Book, and the Slip
Book total did not agree, the clerks would *not* start
at the first break and prove up to that point, and so
on.   They would instead take a break about the
middle, and thus have even chances of finding the
error in the first half or the second half.   Similarly
the work is narrowed down by sub-dividing each
half, if necessary, and so on until the discrepancy is
discovered.   It is, perhaps, hardly necessary to add
that if the mistake affects the higher figures in the
£ column only, the clerks do not trouble about the
shillings and pence, but trace as quickly as possible
the error in the £.   If in the pence column, they do
not trouble about the other columns, and so on.
The object in putting a ring round the figures
marking a "break" is to prevent such figures being
included in the additions.

Before quitting this illustration the reader's
attention is specially drawn to the perfect **absence
of detail. This is one of the cardinal points** of
the system.   No details being necessary there is no
time lost, and it is an undoubted fact that the
taking down of the amounts only does not occupy

COUNTRY DEBITS. April, 1891. SUMMARY.

Day Books	Ledgers	1	2	3	4	5	6	1	8	Totals
1	Genl. O	218 6 9	20 8 6	3 2 6	87 7 7	1691 8 7	365 6 7	17 9 6	420 4 1	2823 14 1
	,, E	12 4 2	384 7 1	191 2 8	4 17 2	816 7 8	45 7 8	1671 2 4	87 7 8	3212 16 5
2	,, O	96 2 7	..	17 6 4	..	45 9 6	..	3462 9 7	..	3621 8 0
	,, E	84 9 1	6 4 6	2716 11 11	88 11 8		910 4 2	241 3 8	640 4 4	4687 9 4
3	,, O	7 6 8	82 8 2	4 6 2	121 1 10	872 18 4	608 7 2	..	96 7 8	1792 16 0
	,, E	172 9 6	18 6 11	..	84 17 6		12 7 6	801 1 9	..	1089 3 2
4	,, O	..	6 8 4	191 1 7	..	976 4 1	111 1 2	76 2 4	121 1 1	1481 19 3
	,, E	18 2 9	..	84 7 9	1971 11 11	27 7 9	49 7 6	..	97 1 2	2247 19 10
5	,, O	1 8 7	..	111 17 6	416 17 2	118 4 2	..	861 2 11	..	1509 4 0
	,, E	961 8 2	490 3 9	..	32 9 4		890 9 9	762 4 2	481 1 11	3617 17 6
6	,, O		156 4 7	384 2 10		84 6 8		81 7 9	37 4 8	748 6 6
	,, E	47 6 2		12 7 8	180 0 2	121 1 4	72 4 1	3 7 6	1191 2 11	1627 9 10
Cash Paid		1618 19 6	1164 11 10	3716 6 11	2987 14 4	4753 8 1	3064 15 7	7977 11 6	3171 16 2	28455 3 11
Transfers		82 9 6		8 14 2	1 11 6	0 1 3		1 118 4	2 1 9	44 14 9
Journal		58 10 ..	3 9 3	..	3 4 3		4 2 6	0 11 1	8 1 6	64 7 3
		1709 19 2	1168 1 1	3725 1 1	2992 10 1	4753 9 4	3068 18 1	7980 0 11	3181 19 5	28579 19 2

any more time than is occupied in calling over without taking down.

No. 4.—COUNTRY DEBITS.

The previous example gave the method of taking down the entries and of making the summary for each Day Book. The present example, which is called "Country Debits," shows the manner in which the totals affecting the various Country Ledgers are brought together from the various books of the Journal class so as to form the totals for each month affecting the debit side of the Country Ledgers. It is compiled from the various Slip Books. The Country Ledgers are assumed to be eight in number, and each Day Book is divided into "odd" and "even" for reasons which will be presently explained. "Cash paid" shown at the foot generally represents such things as dishonoured cheques, small payments made on behalf of customers, or remittances for goods returned. "Transfers" are the totals of the respective columns in the Transfers Book, and probably represent transfers from one account to another, either in the Country Ledgers themselves, or from the Town, Bought, or Private Ledgers. The items marked "Journal" come from the General Journal, usually a private book.

The extreme right-hand column of this table is a collection of the totals recorded in the Slip Books, of which a specimen is given in Illustration No. 2, the items being now arranged horizontally, and the totals in this column of course agreeing with each Day Book. The summary when added up perpendicularly gives the total for the month (April, 1891), of each particular Country Ledger as well as the whole total of all the Country Ledgers.

A separate Book is usually kept to contain the summaries, in order that they may be readily referred to when balancing at the end of the six months, or twelve months, as the case may be.

There are one or two matters in connection with this illustration which it may be as well to refer to, though they form no part of the New Method. They relate to arrangements of the books themselves generally adopted in large concerns to facilitate the work of Book-keeping.

The marks "O." and "E.," meaning odd and even, designate alternate Day Books. On the day when the odd book is being written up by the entering clerks, the even book is being posted into the Ledgers, and thus no time is lost by the ledgerman having to wait till the Day Book can be spared by the entering clerks. The folios are numbered to correspond, thus :—in the odd Day Book the folios run 1, 3, 5, 7, 9, &c., and in the even Day Book 2, 4, 6, 8, 10, and so on. Thus if a reference is made in any Ledger to a Day Book folio, it is plain at once whether it is in the odd book or the even book. It is a common practice to mark these Day Books on the outside—

Monday, Wednesday, and Friday ;

Tuesday, Thursday, and Saturday ;

instead of odd and even, or perhaps in addition thereto.

It is a good plan where there are a number of Ledgers not to commence No. 1 Ledger with a page numbered 1, but number the first page 1000 instead, while Ledger No. 2 commences with 2000, and so on. A clerk using a Ledger, therefore has before him on each page of it, without having to look at the back, a reminder that he is making entries in No. 1 Ledger, No. 2 Ledger, No. 3 Ledger, &c., whenever he sees that the folios commence with 1000, 2000, 3000, &c.

If the accounts of a Company or a Firm are sufficiently voluminous to warrant a monthly proving of the entries, the abstracts taken·from the Ledgers would be agreed with this summary of Country Debits. Debits are usually abstracted separately from Credits. An example of such monthly abstracts is given later on, (in illustrations Nos. 7 and 8,) but as this is no part of the "New Method" we pass on to

No. 5.—COUNTRY CREDITS.

This is the corresponding summary dealing with the Country Credits for the same month as prepared from the slip books. The account books called from are enumerated down the left-hand side of the summary, viz., Cash received, Travellers' Cash (*i.e.* cash collected by the travellers), Country Credits (*i.e.* goods returned, allowances, &c.), Bills Receivable, Transfers, and Journals; everything in fact which is posted to the Credit side of the accounts in the Country Ledgers. The totals at the right hand agree with the monthly totals of each of these books, and the table also defines how much out of the grand total went into each of the eight Ledgers.

No. 6.—COUNTRY LEDGER No. 6 SUMMARY.

This is a summary of the entries affecting the No. 6 Ledger during 6 months, as compiled from time to time from the totals of the Slip Books. In this case it is assumed that the firm or company takes its Balance Sheet every six months, and does not

COUNTRY CREDITS.   April, 1891.   SUMMARY.

Ledgers.	1	2	3	4	5	6	7	8	Totals.
Cash Received	1558 16 5	1671 7 6	1898 14 2	1508 3 10	2322 7 10	2087 3 6	2002 7 9	1886 4 5	15135 5 5
Traveller's Cash ..	430 17 8	380 8 4	897 6 3	550 7 6	928 10 7	663 8 6	535 2 4	987 18 10	5374 0 0
Country Credits....	89 7 6	53 6 3	98 10 1	15 2 1	98 17 3	47 7 10	420 3 10	266 15 6	1089 10 4
Bills Receivable....	405 18 6	364 10 9	448 7 6	383 7 10	323 7 10	409 1 2	512 3 6	405 13 4	3242 10 5
Transfers..........	43 3 8	..	23 16 7	59 18 10	13 17 10	27 10 5	10 7 6	12 3 4	190 18 2
Journal............	5 8 9	8 10 7	26 7 10	..	5 8 10	..	8 10 6	12 5 7	66 12 1
	2533 12 6	2468 3 5	3393 2 5	2517 0 1	3892 10 2	3234 11 5	3488 15 5	3571 1 0	25098 16 5

COUNTRY LEDGER

April.			May.			June.	
	·			··			··
365	6	7	401	11	9	396	16
45	7	8	56	13	9	51	3
		·	62	7	11	92	5
910	4	2	882	5	10	901	16
608	7	2	587	7	6	590	8
12	7	6		··		18	17
111	1	2	99	14	6	105	2
49	7	6	38	2	4	50	2
	··		30	11	8	27	0
890	9	9	460	7	6	532	7
	··		75	3	4	88	11
72	4	1	66	8	10	72	5

SUMMARY for Six Months Account.

CREDITS.	January.			February.			March.			April.			May.			June.			Totals.		
		··			··			··			··			··			··			··	
h Received	1536	7	6	1981	5	3	1026	5	3	1087	3	6	1620	2	3	1901	10	6	9152	14	3
vellers Cash ..	702	5	6	692	10	10	840	17	3	663	8	6	736	10	11	792	18	6	4428	11	6
ntry Credits ..	58	3	5	40	2	7	65	6	6	47	7	10	53	2	8	50	0	8	314	3	8
is Receivable ..	299	17	6	352	17	10	401	6	6	409	1	2	397	11	10	403	5	2	2264	0	0
nsfers	16	10	4	20	11	8	19	3	6	27	10	5	18	19	11	24	5	5	127	1	3
rnals	10	7	8	96	17	6	80	6	5		··		4	6	10	30	18	10	222	17	3
ance 30/6/91....																			5896	6	0
	2623	11	11	3184	5	8	2433	5	5	2234	11	5	2830	14	5	3202	19	1	22405	13	11

prove its entries by monthly abstracts. It is known from the preceding Balance Sheet that when the balances were taken out from this particular Ledger No. 6 the schedule of debtors showed a total of £6132 3s. 10d., and this is the figure with which we start.

Every month, in this case starting with January, the books are called over, and by means of the Slip Books the entries arrange themselves according to the various Ledgers; thereby we find that the total debits for the Country Ledger, No. 6, were during January £2123 3s. 3d., and the total credits £2623 11s. 11d. In a like manner the totals are ascertained for the succeeding five months.

Extending the totals into the outer column on both sides, it is found at the end of the six months that there ought to be balances in the ledger amounting to £5896 6s. 0d. If on taking out the schedule of Debtors in the Ledger the total does not agree the difference has to be traced. It is not however worth while, directly the balances on any particular Ledger have been taken out and tested, to attempt to discover the discrepancy, if any, for it is much better to wait until the same system has been pursued with all the other Ledgers, since it often happens that a corresponding difference is brought out in another Ledger. Thus if one Ledger is, say, £10 15s. 6d. short and another £10 15s. 6d. over, the error may be due to the putting down in the Slip Book of a sum of £10 15s. 6d. under Country Ledger No. 6 instead of Country Ledger No. 7; but it is more likely that in carrying forward a casting to another part of the Slip Book, or carrying it to the Summary, it is put under the wrong Ledger. This naturally does not affect the agreement of the Slip Book with the Journal, as nothing is omitted, but only wrongly placed, and therefore is not discovered until the individual Ledger balances are tested. Where there are differences on several Ledgers, a little calculation will usually indicate the locality of the error.

If it should be necessary to search for an error in a posting to the Ledger which has been passed over in calling, such as an item posted on the wrong side of the Ledger; an item posted in the wrong part of the money column; or a transposition of some of the figures, then in such cases the " New Method " is of very great assistance. For example, take a simple case, if 9/- were posted to the pence column as 9d. the difference in the Trial Balance would be 8/3, consequently it would be necessary to search for all items of 9/- and 9d., and to see that

all such items or other figures ending with 9/- or
9d. had been correctly posted. Under the "New
Method" all that would have to be done would be
to look through the list of items in the slip books
affecting the particular Ledger, instead of having to
search through the whole of the actual Day Books,
Cash Books, etc. The "Breaks" marked in the
slip books easily show where an entry occurs in the
original book.

––––––

The foregoing illustrations are sufficient to show
the general application of the new method, and as
this work is intended for the use of those who have
a more or less expert knowledge of book-keeping,
such as Secretaries of Companies or Counting House
Managers, it would rather tend to cloud the subject
were examples multiplied. No attempt has been
made to carry one set of figures from example to
example, or to weary the reader by taking him
through a whole set of accounts with "New Method"
examples attached, because this would involve a
great number of illustrations and much bulky detail
without any corresponding benefit; hence each
example is given for a different date and consists
of different figures.

Any book-keeper can at once see without further illustration that if every Ledger, whether Town, Country, Bought or Private, is treated in like manner, like results will be obtained, and the summaries thereof will form the total Trial Balance ready for the final Trading, Profit and Loss Accounts and Balance Sheet. Strictly speaking it is only after this has been done that the accounts in the case of the Company should be submitted to audit, but in many cases, especially in private partnerships, the Chartered Accountant employed is often asked to assist in the proving and preparation of the accounts.

The reader has doubtless fully grasped that the central idea of the New Method is that of **turning to practical account a few moments of time hitherto wasted, by putting down figures in any order that may be required.**

IMPORTANT ADVANTAGES ARISING OUT OF THE "NEW METHOD."

Checks upon Fraud, Carelessness, and Indolence.

Detection of the Culprit.

It converts single into double-entry.

Complete and full accounts obtained though books are imperfect.

Cheaper labour utilised.

Flexibility and adaptability of New Method to any sort of accounts.

Can be fully or only partially adopted.

Instance shewing sub-division of accounts in a large firm and of difficulties, in this case, being reduced to $\frac{1}{16}$th.

A Prediction.

This New Method, though originally developed only with the view of obtaining the precise agreement of Trial Balances, is yet found in practical working to be of use in various ways. Some of the remarks bearing upon this part of the subject can be conveniently quoted from the Author's Lecture already referred to, which was given at the Edinburgh Chartered Accountants Students Society.

Check upon Frauds.

"This New Method also involves another point of immense value, and that is that an *employé*, who is perhaps more clever than honest, might, if he were defrauding a firm, ingeniously alter figures after he had observed that they had been examined by the persons checking them, and to which, presumably, they would have no future occasion to refer. If he did so without knowing of, or perhaps appreciating, the full effect of this "taking-down" system, he would infallibly be discovered, as the totals which would be used for the purpose of proving the books would be the unaltered totals shown by the "taking-down" system, and which had been proved to agree with the books as originally written up. Therefore, besides actually discovering the fraud, the "slip-books" would also afford undoubted evidence that at the time the books were called over the particular amount in question was different

from what it appeared as altered. It
should on this account be an invariable
rule that the "taking down" books should
be kept under lock and key by the clerk in
charge of the audit—in fact, in large
audits, a strong box or separate safe is
generally provided for protecting the
checking books, private books, and
memoranda, &c."

Check
upon
Careless-
ness.
"Another element of considerable value
in the " taking-down " system is that where
there are a number of clerks at work it
enables the senior clerk to discover whether
any of the others have done their work
badly, and to detect it every time any
particular journal is called; for, when
the whole of a journal is called, the
casting of the "slip books" must be the
same as that of the journal which has been
called. If not, an error in taking down the
figures, or in adding up the "slip book"
has occurred, and it is at once detected and
the delinquent discovered."

Check
upon
Indolence.
"The senior clerk can also tell whether
any of his men have been idle or have not

made reasonable pace with their work, as by practice it is known how many items a reasonably quick and accurate man can call in a day, and by counting the number of columns filled up in the "slip book" the senior clerk has a record of the clerk's work. There are usually about thirty items in a column."

Detection of Culprit. "When, after a great deal of trouble, an error in the Ledgers which has been passed over in calling is discovered—and such a fault is always serious, though it is easier to occur than might be supposed—the question arises, Who is the culprit? In former times one was dependent upon the manner in which the particular clerk made the regulation tick, and as this, in many instances, had very little individuality, many arguments and disputes arose as to who had ticked the offending item. The "slip book" however settles all such disputes, as the figures made by a clerk are usually as distinguishable from those made by others as the rest of his handwriting."

Flexibility
of System.
"It is not necessary to inaugurate this system in checking every client's books, but only wherever some circumstances render it desirable; at the same time it must not be supposed that it is only valuable in heavy complete audits. It is often used even with very small accounts, especially where the books may be badly kept or in a mess. It has been found of great service in certain classes of Stock Exchange accounts, where it is the exception to find such a thing as a journal. In such cases, transactions are entered direct to the debit or credit of the accounts in the "jobbers ledgers," and again direct to the accounts of the stocks or shares dealt in. The whole book-keeping thus consisting of transfers from one account to another without any intermediate book."

Converts
Single into
Double
Entry.
"The "New Method" is of incalculable value in various investigations, and as a means of converting single-entry books into double-entry as fast as they can be called over."

Complete
accounts
obtainable
though
books
imperfect.

There are other advantages than those quoted above from the Author's lecture. For instance, in making an investigation a Chartered Accountant who is called upon to give a certificate as to past profits, is bound to deal with the accounts as he finds them. They may or may not be in the form that enables him to satisfy himself as to such profits. If they are not in such a form it may be almost impossible for him without the New Method, except at a great expense of time and trouble, to satisfy himself with regard thereto, but if the matter is of sufficient importance to warrant the entries in the books being called over, he is, by adopting the New Method, enabled to obtain in skeleton form any accounts that he may desire duly agreed and balanced, and this as quickly as the entries can be called over.

In other words, no matter how the accounts are kept, or for what purpose it is necessary to check the same, by the New Method one is entirely independent of the form in which any of the books have been kept, and subject to two things :

—(1) that the entries of the transactions that have taken place are truly recorded in some fashion; and (2) that it is worth while to call them—then thoroughly complete and reliable accounts can be obtained from any books whatever.

Cheaper labour utilised. Apart from the greater control over the work already-mentioned, the New Method permits that at least one of the clerks employed may be inexperienced, as if any mistakes are passed over by him when checking, the same are immediately discovered when the Slip Book is agreed with the book from which such clerk has been calling. In this respect it is of mutual value to the employer and to beginners—to the employer as it saves salaries, and to the beginner as he obtains an early knowledge which would otherwise be denied him.

New Method need only be applied partially. It is not necessary to use the New Method throughout the entire system of any firm's accounts, but to adopt it only for such parts where difficulty is experienced.

Instance of Sub-division of Heavy Accounts.   The "New Method" was first inaugura-ted in the Author's Firm some 15 years ago, and the primary idea out of which the system was ultimately developed was mainly conceived by one of their clerks who was engaged upon a very heavy complete audit. No doubt the worry, the bother, and the trouble of having to agree voluminous transactions precisely, led to the inception of the system which has been described. After sub-dividing the books of account, into four main depart-ments, which the nature of the business permitted, then limiting the agreement to one month's figures and agreeing Debits separate from Credits, there were still left indivisible in one of these departments, Fifteen Country Ledgers of 1,000 pages each, full of customers' accounts through-out, and kept in a very hurried manner.

New Method reduces difficulties in this instance to $\frac{1}{15}$th thereof.   These Fifteen Ledgers had to be agreed in one group, as to artificially divide the Day Books, Cash Books, &c. themselves, so as to allocate the entries therein according to each separate ledger was practically impossible, since it would entail a great deal of work and largely interfere with the conduct of the business. When the New Method was developed however, one Ledger could be agreed singly, and consequently there was only **one-fifteenth of the previous trouble** to be experienced.

A
Prediction.

The value of the " New Method " has steadily grown upon the author during the fifteen years' experience he has had of its working, and its utility in so large a number of ways, is such, that he ventures to predict that in course of time there will hardly be any firm of standing—especially those connected with the business of distribution—that will not adopt, in more or less complete form, the New Method. Some little care is perhaps required in adapting the New Method in different cases, but any difficulties, if they should occur, will soon disappear after a little practice and experience of its working, especially if some professional assistance is utilised at the outset.

A MONTHLY PROVING OF BOOKS.

The following explains a style of outside sub-division, somewhat well-known to Chartered Accountants, that does not necessarily entail artificial sub-divisions in the actual books of account, but this system is only useful where the accounts are very heavy and voluminous and warrant the considerable amount of work such a system involves. It therein differs from the New Method, which can be simply and easily applied to any sort of accounts, large or small, either wholly or partially. As this method of monthly proving, however, formed part of the system of accounts mentioned in connection with the audit previously referred to, and it is of a cognate nature to the subject of this work it can properly be included. The following descriptions and illustrations are therefore given.

Where the business transacted is too voluminous to admit of a precise agreement being effected if a Trial Balance is only taken when stock-taking time comes round, intermediate agreements are desirable, and the illustrations here given, Nos. 7 and 8, show

CHECK LEDGER—Example of a Page.

Fo.	Name.	Balance.	Jan.	Feb.	March.	April.	May.	June.	Totals.	Balance.
15	W. E. Addison,	..	3 10 0	8 10 0	10 19 10	8 12 0	5 10 0	4 11 10	36 14 2	4 9 10
	Gravesend		..	7 0 0	7 9 10	8 12 0	..	9 2 6	33 4 4	
21	H. Cross,	19 15 11	4 7 6	9 13 4	20 8 0	85 0 10	8 4 0	8 10 9	101 0 4	33 12 8
	Bromley		10 5 9	9 10 2	6 3 2	10 10 10	16 6 0	14 11 9	67 7 8	
38	F. Bock & Co.,	1 11 4	0 19 2	..	..	7 1 10	5 7 6	10 5 0	25 4 10	15 12 6
	Chatham		..	1 11 4	0 19 2	..	..	7 1 10	9 12 4	
40	J. Burton & Son,	3 2 7	18 10 5	..	3 3 5	8 2 6	1 11 1	..	29 10 0	6 11 1
	Luton		..	4 15 8	2 1 4	1 13 1	12 17 9	1 11 1	22 18 11	
41	J. E. Carrington,	1 15 2	1 13 5	0 7 0	5 5 0	11 14 10	2 2 5	2 15 2	25 13 0	3 7 8
	Strood		1 15 2	1 13 5	..	..	16 3 7	2 13 2	22 5 4	
44	C. Crook,	29 14 4	3 18 7	9 8 8	19 5 5	..	..	6 11 2	68 18 2	15 16 6
	Hastings		16 8 6	13 5 10	6 11 9	1 11 1	9 1 10	6 2 8	53 1 8	
50	F. Churchyard,	18 13 8	17 18 1	8 18 9	19 19 10	..	1 18 6	27 8 5	89 16 10	24 14 0
	Bolton		16 7 9	7 5 1	2 19 8	..	18 11 4	19 19 2	65 2 10	
56	J. Whiffins,	10 12 0	..	..	0 18 9	..	..	..	11 10 9	..
	Windsor		8 14 6	..	1 17 6	0 3 0	0 15 9	..	11 10 9	
78	W. Chapman,		7 10 0	..	..	..	..	..	7 10 0	
	Woking	6 3 0	..	..	1 7 0	..	..	..	7 10 0	
85	F. Barnes,	37 5 0	..	1 0 0	1 17 0	..	..	..	40 2 0	
	Salford		9 0 0	28 5 0	..	2 17 0	..	..	40 3 0	
87	H. Armitage,	38 7 1	10 15 3	..	15 15 5	14 5 3	5 16 2	3 6 8	88 5 10	21 15 6
	Brighton		12 7 1	20 7 9	8 8 1	4 16 8	9 19 0	10 16 9	66 10 4	
118	W. H. Collins,	251 15 7	..	42 10 5	0 14 5	2 12 8	28 1 8	26 3 1	351 17 10	..
	Woking		36 6 11	230 3 7	23 2 9	0 2 0	29 7 5	27 15 2	351 17 10	
119	A. J. Belton,	10 15 8	4 11 8	..	..	..	..	..	15 7 4	..
	Uxbridge		4 2 8	11 4 8	..	..	..	..	15 7 4	
91	R. Barton,		..	..	..	..	..	5 7 10	5 7 10	5 7 10
	Hatfield								..	
126	Jones & Co.,	18 8 11	27 3 7	..	42 15 0	36 19 1	33 4 10	14 5 5	172 16 10	47 10 3
	Hitchin		18 8 11	26 1 7	2 3 0	..	22 17 6	56 16 7	126 6 7	
130	R. Bennett,	..	4 7 6	4 13 0	10 19 0	2 12 6	..	18 17 10	41 9 10	18 17 10
	Watford		..	..	2 12 6	6 8 0	..	13 11 6	22 12 0	
135	Williams & Co.,	4 7 10	..	..	..	..	..	..	4 7 10	4 7 10
	Ealing		4 7 10	..	..	..	..	..	4 7 10	
139	Baldock & Co.,	35 18 0	25 3 4	3 18 8	12 12 0	21 3 3	17 9 0	11 17 5	129 1 8	39 4 8
	Barnet		29 4 6	7 14 8	18 10 0	10 0 6	12 12 8	10 14 11	88 17 5	
		482 2 6	125 8 6	78 19 10	164 13 1	148 4 9	109 5 8	135 0 7	1343 15 1	236 19 11
		6 3 0	167 9 9	367 18 9	88 19 7	40 14 2	149 12 10	180 17 1	1006 15 2	

an excellent way of proving the books each month, as well as of tabulating these monthly figures in such a form that each Ledger balance can be promptly agreed at the date of stock-taking.

The fundamental basis of this procedure is given in a work on Book-keeping by the late Theodore Jones, published very many years ago, the only difference is in a slightly more convenient arrangement. Another form of arrangement, slightly varying from both is given in Mr. G. P. Norton's works, "Textile Manufacturers' Book-keeping," and "Balancing for Expert Book-keepers," which are works published quite recently.

This system of monthly agreements will be understood from a description of each illustration. No. 7 is an example of a page in what is conveniently termed the "Check Ledger," and is supposed to deal with the accounts for sales to Customers of a Firm.

Opposite the name of each customer there are two horizontal lines of figures; the first line represents in black ink the totals on the Dr. side of the account, and the second line, in red ink, represents the totals of the Cr. side of the account. It will be seen that the money columns are so arranged that they commence with the starting balances, and follow on with a column for each month until stock-taking, (in this case assumed to be at the end of six months), and conclude with two final columns to take the totals and balances at stock-taking. Horizontal castings having been made, the totals of both black figures and red figures are carried into the "Totals" column. As we are here dealing with a Sales Ledger the black figures show the total debits for sales, &c., made to the customer, as well as the starting balance, and the total credit figures show the cash, &c., received from him. The difference between these two must necessarily be the balance outstanding at stock-taking. This balance must be agreed with the list of debtors taken out independently from the Ledgers themselves. There is no difficulty whatever in making these agree, as if a balance differs, the monthly figures can be at once compared with the account, and the cause of the difference traced in a few moments.

This illustration is only one page taken out of the book. The reader must imagine that there are a a number of pages in the book sufficient to take all the accounts in the Ledger, and that the totals of each page are carried to the end and summarised. The castings of each page are carried to a summary, instead of being carried forward continuously, as

any correction to be made when balancing will only
affect the total of the page on which it occurs as
well as the one item in the summary, whereas it
would affect all subsequent figures if the castings
were continuous. If for a moment it is assumed
that this example of a page is taken from "Town
Special," then the summary made at the end of this
Check Ledger, will give a total for January debits of
£8681 19s. 1d., February of £6962 4s. 3d., and so
on according to Illustration No. 8.   Therefore,
in the first column "Starting balances," the
summary will show the same total as the list of
debtors.   In the next column, January, the summary
will show in black ink figures the totals of the debit
postings for the month, which of course agree with
the corresponding Day Books, &c., and it will also
show in red ink figures, the total credits for the
month as agreed with the cash received, traveller's
cash, &c.   Though the black and red figures which
appear in each column have to be added up separately,
the colours of the ink are so different that no
difficulty whatever is experienced, and is as easy to
add up either as if the other were not there at all.

The figures shown herein are obtained by going
through the Ledgers monthly, and adding up and
taking out the total debits and credits for each month.

It is to be regretted that the clerk who prepared this example has carefully filled up every line on the page. He ought not to have done so, but should have left some spaces in order that there might be sufficient room to enter a new account if the ledger-keeper should start one on the blank pages between any two existing accounts. He has, however, shown that the ledger clerk did start a new account in June, on folio 91, for " R. Barton Hatfield," and that this account in the Check Ledger had to come after folio 119.

Of course if it were desirable to make agreements for two, three, or more months instead of each month, the same principle would apply, and it would only be necessary to have a less number of columns.

The next illustration (No. 8) gives a **summary of the Check Ledgers and of the Slip Books,** and it shows the working of a monthly agreement together with the totals arrived at by taking down the figures when called by the " New Method." This illustration assumes that there are Nine Ledgers included in the group called " Town Ledgers," and that the Stocktaking period consists of five months, from January to May. Incidentally, it is to be hoped that the totals given for bad debts are

TOWN LEDGERS. Totals from Check Ledgers.

1842. Name.	Starting Balances.			January.			February.			March.			April.			May.		
Town Special	7918	6	0	8681	19	1	6962	4	3	6729	12	10	3690	8	2	2745	14	6
	147	5	1	8100	17	1	7590	6	7	5936	15	2	5589	0	1	4677	7	4
,, 1	7389	8	7	6466	12	10	6567	18	1	7295	19	10	5354	0	8	3481	17	7
	13	12	6	6137	15	8	6431	13	8	7862	5	6	5793	16	8	4693	8	5
,, 2	5552	2	6	4407	6	9	3770	7	0	3999	17	0	3357	1	5	2455	8	6
	207	18	4	4087	8	2	3816	19	3	3816	13	0	4288	10	4	3923	18	7
,, 3	5775	0	4	4067	7	8	5049	2	2	4535	9	8	2747	12	5	1610	0	2
	16	10	10	3964	6	2	4658	4	1	4393	11	4	3867	6	3	3619	16	7
Market	2127	13	4	8476	14	7	8343	11	10	12937	11	10	5931	18	8	12424	8	0
	..			5750	5	3	6824	7	1	11094	0	1	7283	13	4	10283	11	3
Export	4444	2	2	2474	17	11	3189	17	5	3355	8	6	2281	6	1	2572	17	0
	23	1	7	1856	11	2	3950	16	0	2998	10	6	3482	18	9	3173	4	5
Small Accounts	..			..			8	10	6	42	17	5	31	1	5	31	5	9
	..			..			0	4	2	18	13	11	85	14	4	51	10	9
Bad Debts	5945	9	10	..			..			..			..			1712	8	11
	..			150	17	9	20	10	8	94	1	9	113	3	4	2234	2	8
Advertisement	506	18	5	141	18	3	..			..			331	2	10	..		
	13	12	4	52	13	6	21	2	11	26	19	9	106	4	4	849	18	4
	39658	16	2	29716	16	8	33891	11	5	37806	17	1	23724	11	3	27634	0	5
	422	0	8	30100	9	9	35312	4	0	36291	11	0	30561	7	5	33006	18	4

Totals from Slip Books.

Ending Balances.			Starting Balances.			January.			February.			March.			April.			May.			Totals.			Ending Balances.		
3636	13	6	7918	6	0	8681	19	1	6962	4	8	5729	12	10	3690	6	2	2745	14	6	35728	4	10	3636	13	6
..			147	5	1	8100	17	1	7500	6	7	5986	15	2	5589	0	1	4677	7	4	32091	11	4	..		
5623	5	2	7389	8	7	6466	12	10	6567	18	1	7295	19	10	5854	0	8	3481	17	7	36555	17	7	5623	5	2
..			13	12	6	6137	15	8	6431	13	8	7862	5	6	5793	16	8	4603	8	5	30932	12	5	..		
3401	0	6	5552	2	6	4407	6	9	8770	7	0	3999	17	6	3357	1	5	2455	8	6	28542	3	2	3401	0	6
..			207	18	4	4067	3	2	3815	19	3	3816	13	0	4288	10	4	3923	18	7	20141	2	8	..		
3266	16	9	5775	0	4	4067	7	3	5049	2	2	4585	9	8	2747	12	5	1610	0	2	23784	12	0	3266	16	9
..			16	10	10	3964	6	2	4656	4	1	4393	11	4	3867	6	8	3619	16	7	20517	15	3	..		
2007	0	10	2127	18	4	3476	14	7	8843	11	10	12937	11	10	5931	18	3	12424	8	0	45241	17	10	2007	0	10
..			..			5750	5	3	8824	7	1	11094	0	1	7282	13	4	10283	11	3	43294	17	0	..		
2683	6	8	4444	2	2	2474	17	11	3189	17	5	3355	8	6	2281	6	1	2572	17	0	16316	9	1	2683	6	8
..			23	1	7	1856	11	2	3950	16	0	2998	10	6	3482	18	9	3173	4	5	15485	2	5	..		
7	12	1	..			..			8	10	8	42	17	5	31	1	5	31	5	9	113	15	3	7	12	1
..			..			..			0	4	2	18	13	11	35	14	4	51	10	9	106	3	2	..		
5045	3	0	5045	9	10	..			..			..			..			1712	8	11	7657	18	9	5045	3	0
..			..			150	17	9	20	10	3	94	1	9	113	3	4	2234	2	8	2612	15	9	..		
407	3	4	506	13	5	141	18	3	..			..			331	2	10	..			979	14	6	407	3	4
..			13	12	4	52	13	6	21	2	11	26	19	9	108	4	4	349	18	4	572	11	2	..		

more fanciful than the rest of the imaginative figures in this example.

This Summary is built up month by month, and shows at the time of balancing the outstanding accounts on every Ledger, in addition to the monthly proof of the accuracy of the entries. It is built up from two sources which are independent of each other; on the left-hand side, taken from each Check Ledger, in this case nine in all, stand the totals of the individual Check Ledger summaries each month, *i.e.*, the monthly totals from a Check Ledger like that explained in the preceding example, and on the right-hand side the totals independently obtained from the Slip Books of the entries shown therein as the books were called over, as relating to each separate Ledger. If the figures on one side are compared with the corresponding figures on the other, it will be seen that they precisely tally. If, however, the "New Method" is not used, then no agreement of each individual Ledger would appear; only the total of the group of nine Ledgers could be proved. In other words, if only the Check Ledger system were used, the bottom totals commencing on the left-hand with the black figures of £39,658 16s. 2d. and the red figures of £422 ,, — ,, 8d. respectively, could only be agreed *en bloc* month by month with the Journals, and the totals of the "ending balances," £26,228 1s. 10d., could likewise only be agreed *en bloc* with the whole of the Town Ledger balances, but, with the addition of the "New Method" all the numerous figures shown in this illustration can be separately agreed and in consequence a difficulty in obtaining a precise agreement becomes quite unknown.

The ending balances added together make a total of £26,228 1s. 10d. This total must agree with the whole of the balances abstracted from the Town Ledgers and also with the balance of the Town Ledgers Account in the Private Ledger.

In calling over postings where monthly agreements are taken, it is of great value to use different coloured inks for different months, as this facilitates taking out the totals from the Ledgers. The colour of the ink as well as the date helps to define the month's totals in each Ledger Account; if a clerk omits to put a month then the colour detects it.

VARIOUS USEFUL HINTS.

In the course of auditing books and of arranging systems of accounts to suit various businesses, valuable hints and rules are acquired, and it is perhaps not out of place to record a few of them in this work. This list is by no means exhaustive, but includes those only which have occurred to the Author when dictating this book.

Of special application to Chartered Accountants is the rule, that it is requisite to bear in mind the oft-forgotten principle that it is the duty of an expert accountant not to attempt to make a client's business fit his scheme of books, but to make his books fit the client's business, which an expert, if he sufficiently considers the matter, can always find some means of doing.

When calling over is done it should be one of the recognised duties of the ledgerman, who is generally the senior of the two clerks to purposely call back some of the items wrongly, and thereby ascertain whether his fellow clerk is exercising proper vigilance. This is a very wise rule and a stimulus to watchfulness which everyone needs, as a long course of calling over inevitably becomes monotonous, mechanical, and fatiguing. Such a fillip is a capital awakener when skilfully applied.

Another good rule in calling over is that if a clerk's attention is distracted for a moment—say that he is interrupted by someone coming into the room and asking a question—on resuming work it is essential to repeat the last item called, otherwise it might happen to be written down and ticked by the journalman, but not ticked by the ledgerman, or some other inaccuracy occur.

It is well to constantly impress upon clerks the necessity for making very clear figures and placing them under one another, so that they can be readily added up. In this direction illustration No. 3 " How not to do it," may be of service as a visual warning. It is a facsimile of an example given by lime light on the screen during the lecture referred to, and though prepared for a student's lecture, yet as the point is an important one, this object lesson may be again utilised. The addition of the figures has not been attempted. Badly made figures are a fruitful source of differences in a Trial Balance and naturally are one of the first things for which to look. But there are many ways of finding errors that depend on the amount of the difference, such

— Callings — How not to do it. Breaks 136 to 144

46	2	4				26	3	4	500	.	.	
87	3	6	420	5	.	260	13	8	8000	7	6	
245	2	5	42	3	.	60	7	10	80	17	5	
2800	.	.	271		3	4	12	8	2	13	4	
270	.	4	10	10	6	5	14	6	26	13	4	
7	15	.	4	11	8	18	19	11	5	16	3	
18	16	9	22	3	.	6	14	7	57	6	1	
14	3	11	206	7	7	10	14	6	400	11	10	
2	7	3	26	9	3	208	7	3	440	10	11	
26	4	.				28	17	4	6	14	5	
2000	.	.				100	3	10	60	7	1	
200	8	6	(138)			204	18	9	600	4	11	
27	3	4				40	18	11	77	10	3	
100	2	6				10	11	8	776	14	7	
10	3	8	772	10	.	8	10	11	60	2	6	
			72	16	.	7111		4	600	3	5	
(136)			10	18	6	186		11	5	2	6	
			10	8	7	28	5	6	70	15	3	
			350	5	.							
10	12	2	10	11	9	56	7	6	71	2	6	
1000	1	3	5	11	2	32	7	3	4	16	2	
44	11	6	300	4	7	320	17	8	5	6	4	
3	13	9	31	13	3	3000			25	16	3	
20	7	10	40	7	1				28	11	4	
9	19	7							81	1	3/4	
201	4	5				(142)						
2000	.	.										
1000	.	.										
20000	.	.	(140)						(144)			
4	17	6										
2	3	4										
2	14	2										
1	14	2										

as ; looking for half the amount, as the item might
have been put to Dr. instead of Cr. or *vice versa* ;
testing whether it is caused by an amount being put
in a wrong column, for instance, 8/3 might be
caused by 9/- being treated as 9d. ; or whether by
transposition as £210 put as £120 would make a
difference of £90 and so on. Most book-keepers,
however, have learnt by experience these points,
and it is not perhaps useful to amplify instances
herein, though, it is as well to know that very
useful tables of likely errors of transposition, &c.,
arranged in a handy form for immediate reference,
have recently been published in book-form by
Messrs. Gee & Co., of 34, Moorgate Street, E.C.,
the publishers of "The Accountant," entitled
"Errors in Balancing." Its price, 1/- net, is no
measure of its value to the worried book-keeper.

Always adopt the simplest form of entry. Leave
all forms of sub-division other than those into which
the business naturally divides itself to be made by
outside analysis—" the New Method."

Have all account books very carefully planned and
ruled to exactly suit the requirements of the business.
Remember that the stationery used in a book bears
only an insignificant proportion to the cost of labour
in writing it up, therefore for instance, do not

permit the Ledger keeper to create confusion by
carrying forward accounts to various different folios
in order to utilise all the odd bits of space in a Ledger,
as so doing, is in the long run, very expensive.

In all Customers' Ledgers have a space or column
to the right of the debit money column, for the
purpose of making notes as to the statements
and accounts rendered to customers, either of a
temporary nature in pencil or permanently in ink,
as may be desirable. If there is a monthly proving
of books the space should be ruled as a money
column in blue ink.

Do not attempt to rule off the Ledger Account at
each settlement, or to do so at odd times, unless the
transactions with customers are very few and far
between. The better plan is to rule off the Ledger
Accounts once only in each six months or twelve
months, according to the periods for which the
Balance Sheets are taken. The totals on the debit
side less the starting balance will then approximately
give the amount of trade done with each customer
during the given period. This is most valuable
information and should be carefully studied by the
owner or other person responsible for the welfare of
the business concerned.

Every settlement made by the customer can be shown by certain marks, the most convenient of which are the letters of the alphabet. For instance "A" would be put against the cash and discount on the Credit side, represented in the first settlement, and in like manner the letter "A" against the items on the Debit side included in such settlement. Every item included in the second settlement would be marked "B," and every item in the next settlement "C," and so on.

Settlements can be shown by lettering under all circumstances, but an account cannot be ruled off in every instance; where for example a later posted item falls due before an amount posted above it. It is desirable when setting out the money columns of a Ledger to make the pence column wider than usual, so as to leave a space, marked off by a blue line coming after the pence sufficient to take the lettering on both Debit and Credit sides between the blue line and the double red lines that usually close the right hand side of a money column. The letters should be made boldly and in red ink for preference. They should be uniform in size, so that if any item is not settled the vacant space in the lettering column at once strikes the eye.

The responsible head of the business will find it of immense service if at every stock-taking he makes it a rule to go carefully through the schedule of Debtors with his counting house manager, and to take his own notes of those cases where he is not satisfied with the trade done with particular customers, their method of paying, or the credit which they take, also where unsettled claims and disputed items exist, and who is responsible for the non-settlement thereof. Such work renders the Counting House a reproductive department and redeems it from being merely regarded solely as a necessary expense.